TOKENS

"May my thoughts of you ever be
As a bridge to span the space between us."

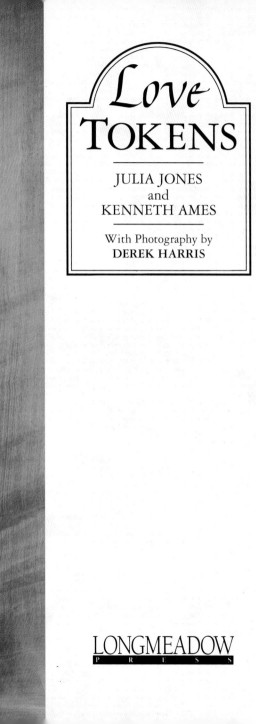

Love TOKENS

JULIA JONES
and
KENNETH AMES

With Photography by
DEREK HARRIS

LONGMEADOW
P R E S S

ACKNOWLEDGEMENTS

The authors and photographer would like to thank the following for their help in producing this book:

Mary Fry, Fulbeck Hall, Lincs; Pamela, Lady Wolseley, Wolseley Bridge, Stafford; Mary Philips of Mary Philips' Antique Jewellery, Wolseley Park Garden Centre, Wolseley Bridge, Stafford; Nancy, Lady Bagot; Perdita and Cordelia Mellor, "Perdy and Cordelia's Antique Shop", Tamworth Street, Lichfield; Pamela Harper, Yvonne Cunningham, Joy Rowe and Barbara Deer.

The authors and photographer have made every effort to obtain copyright permission where necessary on the text and items used in this book. However, should an oversight have been made, this will be corrected in the next edition in this series.

Published by Longmeadow Press,
201 High Ridge Road,
Stamford, CT. 06904

Cover and interior design by Vic Giolitto.

ISBN 0 681 41772 2

Printed in Hong Kong.

First Edition

0 9 8 7 6 5 4 3 2 1

CONTENTS

Love TOKENS

TOKEN: an object that serves to indicate a fact, event or feeling.

The uncertain path of true love is strewn with separations and broken promises, but, with the giving of tokens, love is visibly expressed. The gifts of love take many forms, and in this book we invite you to enjoy their variety and history.

"Send me some token, that my hope may live,
Or that my easeless thoughts may sleep and rest;
Send me some honey to make sweet my hive,
That in my passion I may hope the best.
Send me nor this, nor that, to increase my store,
But swear thou think'st I love thee,
and no more."

JOHN DONNE
"The Token"

VALENTINES

"Blush not, my fair, at what I send,
'Tis a fond present from a friend.
These garters, made of silken twine,
Were fancied by your Valentine.
The motto, dictated by love,
Is simply - Think on what's above."

TRADITIONAL

The Victorian era revived St Valentine as the Saint symbolising love and affection, with the giving of flowers and ornate cards. Old beliefs handed down by word of mouth from Roman times and the influence of the Christian Church have bequeathed us this charming tradition.

The name Valentine derives from the Norman "Galantine", meaning "gallant" or "lover".

St Valentine was said to have worn the birthstone of February in the form of an amethyst ring engraved with a Cupid.

"This visionary theme is thine
From one who loves thee still
Tis writ to thee a valentine
But call it what you will."

GEMSTONES

Gemstones have a greater history and power than is often realised in modern times.

Young girls used to be given aquamarines on their wedding days, as they were believed to combine the auras of the newly-weds and promote harmony and love.

The wearing of a turquoise gemstone was claimed to prevent quarrels between a husband and wife, while a pale sapphire, engraved and set in gold, would procure any desire for its wearer.

Lodestone, though visually less attractive than other gemstones, had the important magnetic power to bring lovers together and for this reason was often featured in Victorian jewellery.

The reddish-yellow stone Padparadschah would be worn to ensure faithfulness.

The blue spinel had the property to cool over-inflamed passions.

Gemstones ruled by Venus, the Roman Goddess of Love, included lapis lazuli, rose quartz, blue diamonds and jade. These should be set in silver or copper. The beautiful blue of the lapis lazuli was thought to strengthen fidelity in love and friendship.

A less well-known stone is the pink rhodochrosite (rhodon - a rose, chrosis - colouring) dedicated to Venus, because of its perfection.

"It is the miller's daughter,
And she is grown so dear, so dear,
That I would be the jewel
That trembles at her ear:
For hid in ringlets day and night,
I'd touch her neck so warm and white.

And I would be the necklace,
And all day long to fall and rise
Upon her balmy bosom,
With her laughter or her sighs:
And I would lie so light, so light,
I scarce should be unclasped at night."

ALFRED, LORD TENNYSON
"The Miller's Daughter"

SHELL VALENTINES

The shells form a mosaic pattern, set under glass, in an octagonal box, which may be hinged to another to make a pair. Often these have a nautical emblem in the design and a motto picked out in shells or seeds.

"Morrow, morrow Valentine
I'll be yours, if you'll be mine
Please give me a Valentine."

"You have a true love on the main,
For love he has ventur'd his life,
But soon will return home again,
And make you his own happy wife."

In the 19th century enterprising locals in the West Indies would assemble shells into kits for sale to visiting sailors. These would be made up on the return voyage to be given to loved ones at home.

"Cupid and my Campaspe played
At cards for kisses; Cupid paid;
He stakes his quiver, bow and arrows,

His mother's doves, and team of sparrows;
Loses them too; then down he throws
The coral of his lip, the rose."

HEART-SHAPED JEWELLERY

Heart-shaped jewellery was worn on the bodice, head, ears, throat and wrists. "The wearing of a heart on the sleeve" to denote affection gave rise to the well-known saying still in use today.

A lover would often wear a red heart cut from fabric or enamelled on to metal, which would then be pinned to the bodice or sleeve.

LOCKET: a small case of gold or silver containing a miniature or a lock of hair.

The giving of a lock of hair has, for centuries, been considered a supreme act of love, as even the possession of a single hair was deemed to give the receiver power over the giver. It was, therefore, a true testimony of love and trust.

"No heart so true
Than mine to you."

20

"Drink to me with only thine eyes
And I will pledge with mine;
Or leave a kiss but in the cup
And I'll not look for wine.
The thirst that from the soul doth rise
Doth ask a drink divine;
But might I of Jove's nectar sup,
I would not change for thine."

BEN JONSON
"To Celia"

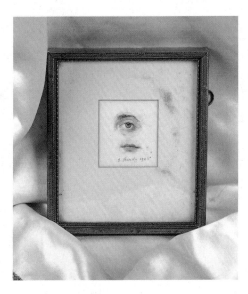

For those who liked to add mystery, tokens were
sometimes given in the form of a miniature paint-
ing of the eye or lips. This would give rise to
much speculation as to whom the "secret one"
might be!

"Let Thee and Me most happy be."

"My heart ye have and thee I crave
I fancy none but thee alone
Wrong not the heart whose joy thou art."

LOVE SPOONS

The custom of giving hand-made wooden or silver spoons as love tokens was widespread in the 17th century.

The symbolism evoked by the way they were neatly stored together, drew the comparison with lovers –

> *"so closely locked together in one another's arms, that it is difficult to move."*

The offering of a love spoon by a suitor and its acceptance or rejection by his beloved gradually developed into a ritual of betrothal, and showed desire to support and protect one's lover.

One heart in a design signified - "my heart is yours." Two hearts showed that both parties felt the same. A chain link attachment usually indicated the number of hoped-for children, while a comma represented the soul.

"Without your sweet token
of love's distant fire,
I know that my heart
would surely expire."

"Your token's my comfort,
Until you return
In this lonely heart
A fire will burn."

SAILORS' TOKENS

Stay or corset busks were often carved in wood by a lover for his sweetheart. Busks seemed a natural subject for love tokens, as they formed an intimate part of the wearer's apparel, being so close to the heart. Many ivory stays and busks were made on board ship for loved ones at home.

Glass rolling pins were also popular tokens, and would usually bear a rhyme.

"If you loves I
As I loves you
No pair so happy
As we two."

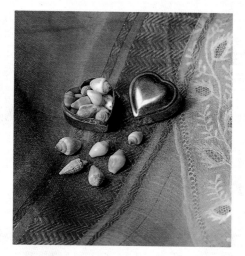

"Eliza kiss me quick
And don't be shy
For you love kissing, dear,
As well as I."

Sailors would send elaborately tasselled, heart-shaped pincushions, decorated with mother-of-pearl buttons, pinheads and sequins, and bearing a loving message.

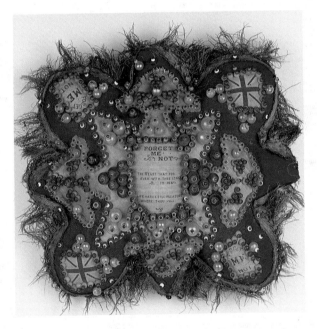

"My sweetheart's a Sailor,
He sails on the sea,
When he comes home
He brings presents for me;
Coral from China,
Silks from Siam,
Parrots and pearls
From Seringapatam,
Silver from Mexico,
Gold from Peru,
Indian feathers,
From Kalamazoo,
Scents from Sumatra,
Mantillas from Spain,
A fisherman's float,
From the waters of Maine,
Reindeers from Lapland,
Ducks from Bombay,
A unicorn's horn
From the Land of Cathay -
Isn't it lucky
For someone like me
To marry a Sailor
Who sails on the sea!"

ELEANOR FARJEON
"Sailor"

"Then in his arms he will clasp me and I
For him will live — though for him I could die,
What a sweet world is this! Now I have found
What it is — love it is — makes it go round."

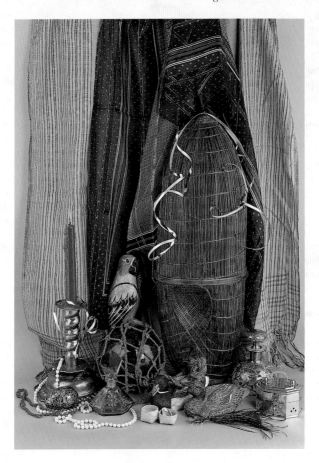

PINCUSHIONS

For several hundred years pincushions were made by girls as tokens of affection. These usually incorporated an appropriate inscription, the couple's initials and the date. In Victorian times, a pincushion in the shape of a pansy or heartsease was considered a suitable gift for a girl to give a young man.

> _"I gave thee a paper of pins_
> _Another time a tawdry lace_
> _And if thou wilt not be my love_
> _Indeed I'll die before your face!"_

TRADITIONAL

The original colours of the pansy – purple, yellow and white – symbolised to the French "memories, souvenirs and loving thoughts".

LACE BOBBINS

The long wearisome day of the lacemaker would be lightened by the constant presence of the lover's gift of an inscribed bobbin on her lace pillow. The inscriptions on lace bobbins expressed a whole range of human emotions, and were much prized by their owners.

"This ring is round
And so is a shilling.
I am ready
When you are willing."

34

Twenty-four hand-carved bobbins were considered a fitting gift for a Devon boy to offer his sweetheart on Valentine's Day.

"My love don't list"

This from a girl who did not wish her lover to enlist as a soldier.

"Give me a kiss for a token."

"Kiss me, court me, hug me tight
Pray don't crump my collar tonight."

L E T T E R S

"More than kisses, letters mingle souls."

JOHN DONNE

Robert Browning to Elizabeth Barrett:
2nd May, 1846

So now, at $2^1/2$ p.m., I must (- here is the
Post......from you?) Yes - the letter is here at last -
I was waiting: - now to read; no, kissing it comes
first.

Elizabeth Barrett to Robert Browning:
12th May, 1846
Look what is inside of this letter - look! I gathered it for you today when I was walking in the
Regent's Park...the sun was shining with that
green light through the trees...and I put both my
feet on the grass...which was the strangest feeling!
and gathered this laburnum for you.

"An exquisite invention this,
Worthy of Love's most honeyed kiss -
This art of writing billet-doux
In buds and odours and bright hues!
In saying all one feels and thinks
In clever daffodils and pinks;
In puns of tulips, and in phrases,
Charming for their truth of daisies."

LEIGH HUNT
"Love Letters Made of Flowers"

FLOWERS

O ver the centuries an elaborate language of
flowers has evolved.

No flower was said to be without meaning and
it was possible to send messages of passion without even inking the page.

If a young girl was presented with a sprig of
the plant "lad's love" she would accept the young
man's favour by smelling the sprig. To throw it
away would reject his advances.

*"Then the two passed round to the rose trees,
where he gathered blossoms and gave her to
put in her bosom. She obeyed like one in a
dream, and when she could affix no more, he
himself tucked a bud or two in her hat, and
heaped her basket with others in the
prodigality of his bounty."*

THOMAS HARDY
"Tess of the d'Urbervilles"

"Here's ivy! - take them, as I used to do
Thy flowers, and keep them where
they shall not pine.
Instruct thine eyes to keep their colours true,
And tell thy soul their roots are left in mine."

ELIZABETH BARRETT BROWNING
"Sonnets from the Portuguese"

"There is a language, 'little known',
Lovers claim it as their own.
Its symbols smile upon the land,
Wrought by Nature's wond'rous hand;
And in their silent beauty speak,
Of life and joy, to those who seek
For Love Divine and sunny hours
In the language of the flowers."

F.W.H

GEMMEL RINGS

"Thou sent'st to me a true love-knot,
but I,
Returned a ring of jimmals to imply
Thy love had one knot, mine a triple tie."

ROBERT HERRICK
"The Jimmall Ring or True Love Knot"

G emmel rings were extremely popular in Elizabethan times. The word "gemmel" means "jointed hinge" and refers to the fact that these rings were made in two or three interlocking sections.

When two people became engaged, they would break the ring over an open bible. Each would then take their part, only to reassemble it at the wedding ceremony.

"Young girls grow eager as the day retires
And smile and whisper round their cottage fires
Listening for noises in the dusky street.
For tinkling latches and for passing feet
The prophecys of coming joys to hark
Of wandering lovers stealing thro' the dark
Dropping their valentines at beauty's door
With hearts and darts and love knots littered o'er."

JOHN CLARE

41

LOVE KNOT

The age old significance of knot-tying has long held a great influence in the cementing of relationships. To tie a knot represents the binding or holding of one to another and strengthens love and marriage, preventing the intervention of evil-doers. In many parts of the world, the wedding ceremony itself involves a whole series of knot-tyings. At the Tudor court a love knot would be cut from gold fabric and sewn to a Valentine costume, denoting that the wearer's affections were engaged.

In rural areas a true lover's knot or straw token might be made by a young man to give to his maid. If she pinned this over her heart, it indicated that she had chosen him, and the token would be worn until their wedding day.

The love knot, without beginning or end, is an ancient symbol of everlasting love, and at weddings blue love knots would be given to denote constancy.

A lad's straw token would be offered with the grain attached, as a symbol of female fertility. Girls would remove the grain from the tokens they gave the boys.

"She stood breast high amid the corn
    Clasp'd by the golden light of morn,
        Like the sweetheart of the sun,
    Who many a glowing kiss had won.

Sure, I said, Heav'n did not mean,
Where I reap thou shouldst but glean,
    Lay thy sheaf adown and come,
    Share my harvest and my home."

THOMAS HOOD
"Ruth"

"*True love is a precious pleasure,*
Rich delight unvalued treasure,
Two firm hearts in one meeting,
Grasping hand in hand ne'er fleeting,
Wreath-like like a maze entwining,
Two fair minds in one combining,
Foe to faithless vows perfidious."

In its original form this illustration was first
published in London in 1641.

"True love is a knot religious,
Dead to the sins and flaming rise
Through beauties soul seducing eyes,
Deaf to gold enchanting witches
Love for virtue not for riches.
Such is true loves boundless measure,
True love is a precious pleasure."

THE FOODS OF LOVE

The sharing of food and drink by lovers has for centuries been represented in song and literature, both for its symbolism and its aphrodisiac quality.

"D'Urberville began gathering specimens of fruit for her, handing them back to her as he stooped; and presently, selecting a specially fine produce of the 'British Queen' variety, he stood up and held the stem to her mouth.

'No - no!' she said quickly, putting her fingers between his hand and her lips. 'I would rather take it in my own hand -.'

'Nonsense!' he insisted; and in a slight distress she parted her lips and took it in."

THOMAS HARDY
"Tess of the d'Urbervilles"

46

"I gave her cakes and I gave her ale
And I gave her sack and sherry
I kist her once and I kist her twice
And we were wondrous merry."

HENRY PURCELL
"I Gave Her Cakes
And I Gave Her Ale"

"*And still she slept an azure-lidded sleep,*
In blanchéd linen, smooth and lavender'd,
While he from forth the closet brought a heap
Of candied apple, quince, and plum,
and gourd."

"With jellies soother than the creamy curd,
And lucent syrops, tinct with cinnamon;
Manna and dates, in argosy transferr'd
From Fez; and spiced dainties, everyone,
From silken Samarcand to cedar'd Lebanon."

JOHN KEATS
"The Eve of St Agnes"

CHASTITY RINGS

The abiding strength of love was measured by some in observing the lasting qualities of these rings. The belief being stated in the engraving –

"When this ring grows pale and wan
You may know by it my love has gone."

ETERNITY RINGS

"Letters, lockets, pictures and rings."

RICHARD CONGREVE
Tattle's proof of his conquests
"Love for Love"

The first Victorian eternity rings always included at least one garnet as a symbol of constancy and fidelity.

GIARDINETTO RINGS

The Italian "small garden" or Giardinetto ring, with delicate floral designs, was a favourite token of the wealthier 17th century suitor for his beloved.

"Oh! Love may be given
And love may be spoken
But I seek a love
That is sealed with a token.
A locket, a ring, or a fine precious stone
And then will I know
That your love is my own."

REGARD RINGS

Victorian regard rings were set with a Ruby, Emerald, Garnet, Amethyst, another Ruby and finally a Diamond. The first letters of each stone spelling the sentiment "regard".

These stones endowed the wearer with their own special powers.

The ruby was said to cure any evil that might spring from love or friendship.

The emerald was an emblem of success in love.

For those born in January, the wearing of their birthstone, the garnet, was thought to grant fidelity, truth and happiness.

The amethyst next, for its associations with Venus, one more ruby, then a diamond, the stone of reconciliation, which was also said to encourage marital harmony.

*"May the Lord watch between me and thee
when we are absent one from another."*

GENESIS XXXI v. 49

Mizpah rings were often given as talismans to
departing soldiers; the name implying watchful-
ness by the donor.

ENGAGEMENT RINGS

"A simple ring with a simple stone
To the vulgar eye no stone of price:
Whisper the right word, that alone -
Forth starts a sprite, like fire from ice."

ROBERT BROWNING
"A Pearl - A Girl"

An opal is still considered unlucky in an engagement ring, as are pearls, for should they be given to a woman about to be married they would bring her "a torrent of tears".

The circle has long been a symbol of eternity. This harks back to man's early belief that to encircle his partner would bind her to him. This magic circle would also enable his spirit to enter her body. Originally this circle would have been of rope. The ring was also considered an amulet to ward off evil. The wedding ring was a development from the engagement ring and was used as a token to ward off other suitors.

"First time he kissed me, he but only kissed
The fingers of this hand wherewith I write
And ever since, it grew more clean and white
Slow to world-greetings, quick with
its 'Oh List'
Where the angels speak a ring of amethyst
I could not wear here, plainer in my sight
That that first kiss, the second passed
in height."

ELIZABETH BARRET BROWNING
"Sonnets from the Portuguese"

WEDDING RINGS

"The ring so worn as you behold,
So thin, so pale, is yet of gold;
The passion such it was to prove;
Worn with life's cares, love yet was love."

GEORGE CRABBE
"A Marriage Ring"

I n Medieval times the wedding ceremony was held in the porch of the church. The priest would first place the wedding ring on the top of the left thumb, which represented God. It was then moved to the first finger to indicate Jesus Christ the Mediator, and then to the middle finger symbolising the Holy Spirit. Finally, it would be actually worn on the third finger of the left hand. The intention was that the groom should devote his life to his spouse, after the Holy Trinity – his wife being represented by the third finger.

"I love thee — I love thee!
'Tis all that I can say; —
It is my vision in the night,
My dreaming in the day;
The very echo of my heart,
The blessing when I pray;
I love thee — I love thee!
Is all that I can say."

"Thy bright and hazel glance,
The mellow lute upon these lips,
Whose tender tones entrance;
But most, dear heart of hearts, thy proofs
That still these words enhance,
I love thee — I love thee!
Whatever be thy chance."

WEDDING
FAVOURS

Bride favours were given out as tokens before or after the ceremony. These were in the form of topknots, garters or even small baskets to hang in the house.

The figures on a wedding cake are also ancient fertility tokens, as is the cake itself.

Gifts given to the bride from the groom were known as "Corbeille". These gifts should be of gold, which is ruled by the masculine sign of the sun.

Bride's gifts to the bridegroom were usually of silver, this being under the lunar, and therefore, feminine influence.

> *"As silver meets gold*
> *And a new day's begun,*
> *Then I am the moon*
> *And you are the sun...."*

"Ask nothing more of me, sweet;
All I can give you I give.
Heart of my heart, were it more,
More would be laid at your feet:
Love that should help you to live,
Song that should spur you to soar.

All things were nothing to give
Once to have sense of you more,
Touch you and taste of you, sweet,
Think you and breathe you and live,
Swept of your wings as they soar
Trodden by chance of your feet.

I that have love and no more
Give you but love of you, sweet:
He that hath more, let him give;
He that hath wings let him soar;
Mine is the heart at your feet
Here, that must love you to live."

ALGERNON SWINBURNE
"The Oblation"